About the Book

Shirley Mathis was raised by her mother in rural, segregated Georgia. As a Black child in a small southern town, she met prejudice in many forms. She went on to become the first Black person to earn a doctorate from the University of Georgia. Her doctorate is in mathematics. Shirley Mathis McBay is now Dean for Student Affairs at the Massachusetts Institute of Technology.

This is the story of a girl who loved math, who had a goal, and who always understood that giving in to peer pressure was not going to get her where she wanted to go.

an American Women in Science biography

Mathematician and Administrator,

Shirley Mathis McBay

by Mary Ellen Verheyden-Hilliard

drawings by Scarlet Biro

The Equity Institute
Bethesda, Maryland

 Published in the United States by The Equity Institute, P.O. Box 30245, Bethesda, Maryland 20814.

This work was developed under a grant from the Women's Educational Equity Act Program, U.S. Department of Education. However, the content does not necessarily reflect the position of that Agency and no official endorsement of these materials should be inferred.

Library of Congress Cataloging in Publication Data

Verheyden-Hilliard, Mary Ellen.
Mathematician and administrator, Shirley Mathis McBay.

(An American women in science biography)

Summary: A brief biography of the woman mathematician who was the first Afro-American to earn a Ph.D. from the University of Georgia.

1. McBay, Shirley Mathis—Juvenile literature. 2. Afro-American mathematicians—Biography—Juvenile literature. 3. Afro-American college administrators—Biography—Juvenile literature. [1. McBay, Shirley Mathis. 2. Mathematicians. 3. Afro-Americans—Biography] I. Biro, Scarlet, ill. II. Title. III. Series: Verheyden-Hilliard, Mary Ellen. American women in science biography.

QA29.M38V47 1985 510'.92'4[B][92] 84-25983
ISBN 0-932469-04-3

Mathematician and Administrator,

Shirley Mathis McBay

"Mirror, mirror on the wall, who is the fairest of them all?"

The school play was going well. As 10-year-old Shirley Mathis spoke the words of the queen, she raised her arms above her head. She seemed to command an answer from the mirror. Shirley liked playing the queen. The queen did not sit around and wait to be rescued. Shirley did not like to sit around either.

At the end of the play, the audience clapped. Shirley and her classmates were a hit!

That night Shirley took her bath in the tin tub. "Mama, the water's getting cold." Her house had a bathroom but not a bathtub.

Shirley's mother brought another kettle of hot water from the stove. She poured it into the soapsuds.

"The math contest is tomorrow, Mama," Shirley said.

Her mother smiled. "Finish your bath. We'll talk on the porch. I'll be done with the dishes by then." Shirley's mother worked as a maid. That job did not pay very much. To get a little more money for Shirley and herself, she also rented rooms in their house.

Later, out on the porch, Shirley and her mother sat in the old swing. "The math contest is between you and a high school student, isn't it?" her mother asked.

"Yes, but if I put my mind to it, I'll win." Shirley liked math. That was not the problem.

The swing moved quietly back and forth. "You know, Mama, sometimes the kids tease me. They don't see any sense in studying."

"I know," her mother said.

"But learning things makes me feel good." Just saying it aloud made Shirley feel better.

"And will you feel good tomorrow when you win?" her mother asked.

Shirley began to smile again. "I'll feel great!"

Jj Kk Ll Mm Nn Oo Pp Qq Rr Ss

The next day, Shirley's teacher had everything ready. Shirley stood on a chair at the chalkboard. That gave her the same space to work as the high school student, who was much taller.

The math problems were hard. Shirley did them all. When she finished, she looked around. She had finished first. Her teacher checked the answers. Shirley's were all correct!

When school was out, Shirley ran all the way home. She sat on the porch swing waiting for her mother to come from work.

As soon as she saw her mother, she ran to her. "I did it, Mama, I won!"

Shirley was born on May 4, 1935. She had lived all her life in Bainbridge, Georgia. Shirley and her mother had very little money. Her mother thought Shirley would have a better chance if she lived with relatives in Chicago. So when she was in the sixth grade, Shirley went to Chicago.

Shirley liked her new school. Her teacher was nice. Sometimes, just like back home, the other girls and boys teased her because she liked to study. But that didn't stop Shirley. In her new class, the student with the best grades got to sit in the first chair of the first row of seats. Soon Shirley was sitting in that seat.

But Shirley was lonesome for home. When she was doing math, she was happy. But when school was over and her homework was done, she wished she were back home. She wished she could swing in the old swing. She wished she could talk with her mother.

Shirley did go back home. There still wasn't much money, but Shirley was happy.

One day Shirley read in the newspaper about a company that hired women to sell lipstick and perfume door-to-door. Shirley told her mother about it. Her mother decided to try to get the job.

Shirley wrote a letter for her mother asking for the job. Her mother was hired. Shirley's mother was a good salesperson. People liked to talk with her. The company liked the way she did her work. The extra money was a big help. Life became a little easier.

When Shirley was in high school, she walked a mile and a half to get to the school for Black students. The long walk took her past the park. The park was pretty and green. She wished she could walk through the park. But that was one risk Shirley knew she could not take, because she was Black. In Bainbridge, Georgia, in the 1950's, only white people were allowed to walk in the park.

As she walked along the side of the park, she remembered her cousin Elizabeth.

When Elizabeth was 17 years old, she went to the dime store to buy a comb. A white boy came up and spit on her for no reason. Elizabeth got mad and hit him. Elizabeth had to leave town in a hurry so she would not be hurt. Back then, Black people were not supposed to fight back, no matter what was done to them.

Shirley and her mother had gone to her cousin's house to help her pack. Elizabeth went to an aunt's house in Florida. It had been a scary time.

Shirley had fun in high school. She was a cheerleader. She acted in school plays. And she still liked math.

Sometimes her friends still tried to get her to forget about school work. Many girls and boys didn't see any point to studying. But Shirley believed what her mother told her—a good education would help her all her life.

Shirley's teachers helped her too. They lent her books. They helped her write letters to colleges to find out how much it would cost to go to college.

Shirley went to Paine College. She had good grades, so she won a scholarship. She also earned money working as a waitress in the college dining room. She worked at breakfast, lunch, and dinner. In between, she went to classes and studied.

In her first year at college, Shirley took a very hard math class. All the students were older than Shirley. But it was Shirley who earned the only "A" grade in the class!

Later on in college, Shirley got a job as a secretary. She worked in the office of the president of the college. She had a chance to meet and talk with interesting people who visited the president.

When Shirley graduated from college, she had the highest grades in her class.

After college, life got even busier for Shirley. She met and married Dr. Henry McBay, a chemistry professor. She started taking advanced science courses. She taught at Spelman College, a college for Black women. As the years passed, she and her husband had two sons, Michael and Ronald.

Shirley became the first Black person to earn a doctorate from the University of Georgia. A doctorate is the highest degree a scientist or scholar can earn. Her degree is in mathematics. The university asked her to come and be the first Black person to teach in the math department at the university.

But Shirley decided to continue teaching at Spelman. Because of the work she did at Spelman, many young women decided to major in science and math.

In the next few years, Shirley and her husband began to drift apart. After much thought, they decided to divorce. Michael and Ronald stayed with their mother, but they saw their father often.

Shirley's success in encouraging Black women to study science was noticed by the National Science Foundation in Washington, D.C. She went to work for the Foundation. Her job was to help colleges encourage minority students to become scientists.

Shirley liked her work. Her two sons were doing well. One was studying business. The other was studying medicine. Shirley's mother is also doing well. She is

87 years old. Although she does not have to work now, she still

enjoys selling beauty products for the same company.

Dr. Shirley Mathis McBay now works at the Massachusetts Institute of Technology. She is Dean for Student Affairs. She directs a staff of 35 people.

Dr. McBay says that having learned how to solve problems in math and science helps her in her work. It helps her think clearly in solving problems in her new career.

To the young women and men who come to her for advice, Dr. McBay shares what she learned when she was a little girl.

"Study hard, whether your friends do or not. And always

believe in yourself. Remember, if you don't *try* you'll never know if you can *succeed.*"

Verheyden-Hilliard,
Mary Ellen
Mathematician and
administrator,
Shirley Mathis McBay